YOLANDA

An Oral History In Verse

poems by

Tim Tomlinson

Finishing Line Press
Georgetown, Kentucky

YOLANDA

An Oral History In Verse

ACKNOWLEDGMENTS

My wife, Deedle Rodriguez-Tomlinson, accompanied me on every step of the research-gathering
component of this project. She translated the Tagalog that came up in interviews, and on
transcripts. She shot a significant percentage of the photographs that we gathered to document
the work. She helped with the transcription of the field recordings. She toughed it through many
trying situations. Without Deedle, the work could not have been done.

The help and guidance of Joycie Dorado Alegre, Director of the University of the Philippines Leyte-
Samar Heritage Center, was invaluable in all our on-site work. She helped with subjects, protocols,
practices—with the tangible (accommodations, transportation) and the intangible (the spirit of
delicate interactions). Joycie's spirit informs this collection; without it, the book would not be.

Popo Tabao Amascual provided company, insight, context, and relentlessly self-sacrificing
assistance. He conducted the Waray-Waray interviews. He was a resource in every way possible,
available at any time. Popo's spirit, too, informs this collection.

At the University of the Philippines-Visayas, in Tacloban, Dean Anita Garrido Cular provided space,
time, and transportation. Assistant Dean Birdie Lorenzo helped with stories and transportation.

Danica Arriesgado and Le-an Lacaba provided nuanced translations of Waray-Waray interviews.
Their transcriptions were critical in the formation of the resulting poems.

Sarah Drepaul transcribed many difficult tapes.

Special thanks to Dean Fred Schwarzbach, Global Liberal Studies, New York University, whose
generous assistance enabled everything that followed.

Michele Y. Dee, of the AY Foundation, also provided generous assistance.

Finally, my heartfelt thanks to the interview subjects, whose stories were epic in courage and
pathos, and whose articulation of those stories provides the heart and soul of this collection.

"The People Started Walking" appeared in Red Paint Hill, Issue #7

Editor: Christen Kincaid
Cover Art: Tim Tomlinson
Author Photo: Robert L. Lascaro, Design Factory
Cover Design: Elizabeth Maines

Printed in the USA on acid-free paper.
Order online: www.finishinglinepress.com
            also available on amazon.com

Author inquiries and mail orders:
Finishing Line Press
P. O. Box 1626
Georgetown, Kentucky 40324
U. S. A.

Table of Contents

AN ORAL HISTORY IN VERSE OF
SUPER-TYPHOON HAIYAN/YOLANDA
LEYTE-SAMAR, PHILIPPINES—NOVEMBER 2013

FISHES JUMPING ON THE STONES (NARRA SERDINA, 73, BARANGAY 69, NOV 8, 2013)

I was born here. I gave birth here.

I prayed the rosary in the morning,
and my niece told me, "Mama, look, the water backed up far away."

"You're a liar," I told her. "Let me see."

And I saw
         the fishes jumping on the stones.
I told her the water will be big.

I went home and the water came with me.

THE STORM (FATHER HECTOR, SAN JOSE NOV 8 2013)

When the water came
I was alone hiding, taking cover,
anticipating that the roofing might not hold,
worried of dying.

The water came
the strong winds howling, shaking the whole place,
white mist like needles piercing through my skin.
I'm going to die in this place.

Later our neighbors came
scampering climbing shouting panicking.
This is okay, this is good—
there's somebody to tell my relatives

I died this way.

THE STORM (BERT TUAZON, SUPT REGIONAL POLICE, PALO, NOV 8 2013)

five in the morning the storm hit
the strong wind
our roof taken one by one

we cornered into our tactical operation center at the 2nd floor
twelve to fifteen in the small room
hide under the table we told them
I wasn't sure if we were going to survive
I don't know if it was secure

our regional director was holding a baby
a four year old baby
and they were covered by policemen

our room was getting gutted
our roof falling the ceiling falling
I placed myself on the wall

I used the stool to cover my face
never mind that my whole body will be wet
the other policemen covered the windows
with foam so we will not be blown away

so in that two hours or three hours
we could not do anything

three times we attempted to go to the 1st floor
but we could not see anything
only white

EVACUATION AND RETURN (PELEGRINA EGANA, 55, BARANGAY 69, NOV 8-10, 2013)

that night a vehicle urged everyone to evacuate
mother had difficulty walking so we didn't go

mother kept saying let's stay here nothing will happen
early in the morning, half of our house was gone

we didn't know what was happening we just closed our eyes
screaming "Water! Huge water!"

the rain stinging our eyes like there was sand with it
everyone started to run

Let's run everyone! To the mountains let's run!
I looked back the barge was already there

so we ran dragging our mother up
on the mountain there wasn't any roofs or wood flying around

being swept away by the wind
we held on to a tree

having cramps because of how long we held on
my mother pitiful drenched shaking

when the storm subsided, our house was nothing,
even the walls, nothing. We picked up some pieces,

some things we found. We didn't eat for two days
only biscuits from whoever was willing to give

we'd even drink the rainwater
The dead just there, passed by.

We make a home out of the wood,
sleeping under there on leaves.

Mother died after two months, scared.

The barge is still on our house.

THE BARGE (SERAPHIM PEDROSA, 76 YEARS OLD, BARANGAY 69, NOV 9, 2013)

we were asleep
around six in the morning
something flew by and hit one of my windows
someone said, "tatay, water"
the next thing the water
was at waist level

we saw the barge
as well as the darkening of the world
my house was nothing
the barge was on top of our house
and the houses were gone
my house it was nothing anymore
a little portion of a steel bar

the barge
right there in the center
the center of the barge
the barge was the one that destroyed our home
until now it's there like an exhibit
the floor of my house
is still there

EVIDENCE (DULZ CUNA, SAN JOSE, NOV 8 2013)

we were expecting it, the news—
        people evacuating when
the rain started and the wind—
        I prepared my windows, like that
with tarpaulins but the rain came—
        the bedroom the whole room the sala
a virtual washing machine—
        everything flying around

the wind could blow you against the wall—
        the tornado inside the room
the tarpaulin burst out, the screen—
        flew all over the room and water
on the second floor our little flood—
        downstairs flooded to the ceiling
the two people living downstairs—
        they had to swim, they had to crawl

clutching my daughter, rosary beads—
        and a cell phone. I told my daughter
I better take pictures, you know—
        of the room ... they find our bodies
drowned like rats at least the cell phone—
        would show how we died waterlogged
Mommy you're ridiculous—
        she kept saying because, just hold on

I was thinking of my father—
        he was a judge, a lawyer.
"Always have evidence," so—
        I took pictures, with my cell phone.
Howl 1. Howl 2. Howl 3. Yes.—
        I posted them on Facebook.
If they were going to take us—
        at least I have evidence.

THE GIANT CLAW (BEATRICE ZABALA, 16, PALO, NOV 8, 2013)

Before the giant claw came, I was inside
the comfort room with my grandmother.
She was praying the whole time. My parents
called us to transfer to a safer room,
but the winds kicked up, slamming on our door.
The wind was like a drunken man punching
the door, kicking it, trying to rip it apart.
The strong winds against my father's strength.

Then suddenly, I felt water on the floor.
I thought fresh water from the river, it
didn't smell salty. It started to rise,
to our knees, our waist, our chin. Salt water.
How was it possible? The sea was almost
a kilometer away! Then, the giant claw came.

THE WALL (JULITO SANCHEZ, 48, LABORER, ANIBONG, NOV 8, 2013)

The wind started to gather strength,
blowing past my ears, getting stronger and stronger.
Everything was flying outside, tin roofs like missiles.
I tried to see the church,
      all I could see was white.

We huddled inside a small room, all of us, my family, terrified.
Looking at them, it tears my heart, it rips my remaining courage
      to pieces.
My children so scared, cowering in that little corner of the room,
      eight of them.
I should be strong for them. I am the father.
My wife strangely silent, her face shocked.

The wall across us has an image of Jesus, a poster.
And my children were staring at it, looking at the image,
      crying, screaming, calling His name. *"Papa Jesus! Papa Jesus!"*
I was afraid, so afraid.
My wife was panicky, urging me to transfer to a safer place.
I told her, no we're staying here. The walls on this side are stronger.
I could never risk the safety of my family,
      crossing the space to look for another building.
No matter what happens, I told them, we should stay together.

And then the wall started to move.

THE SURGE (ZENIA DULCE, 46, PROFESSOR UP VISAYAS. TACLOBAN, NOV 8, 2013)

I called to her,
I called to her and then
we held each other's hand

and then suddenly the water under her
inside the house it was eating up the whole house
and she said oh my god

and then suddenly
one wave washed her down then another wave
another wave brought her up

so I held her
another wave put us both down together
with the whole house

so all the house and us we were under
and we did not know what was happening to us
but we held on together

we are both safe she knows because I am holding on to her
I give her a signal to hold on tightly
and then we were engulfed by the water

and then we tried to go up
once we neared the surface I released her
so that we would be able to have the chance to crawl up and swim

well the water was actually pushing us up together
I was telling her to it's OK you release
so she released her hold on me also

and we resurfaced but the problem
we were both trapped big debris uh, maybe big debris
like this four or six like this

I don't know it's big I was scratched
this is still the bruise uh what do you call this my remembrance
and that was how many months ago that was six months
            eight months ago

and that bruise is still there
I was struck here also at my back
and she was struck at the neck I heard the snap

like that super loud
and then there was no emotion on her face
I saw the blood blood blood coming out from her nose and mouth

I thought oh my god she's dead
and then slowly slowly
she was sinking

THE MIDDLE OF THE OCEAN (LUCY ZABALA, 46, PALO, NOV 8, 2013)

It felt like the middle of an ocean.
I kept paddling but the water kept dragging
me under so I had to breathe again,
gasping. On my way up, I saw the surface
covered with floating debris. I was trapped!
I thought I would really die. There were three waves,
I couldn't forget that because I went down
three times. When I tried to catch for breath,
the waves would slam and pull me down again.
It was just a matter of seconds, before
the next wave came. Then I saw floating wood,
a trunk as big as my leg. I clung to it.
I told myself I would stay with this trunk,
I would go wherever it takes me.

THE CROSS (DR ROSARIO LATORRE, TACLOBAN NOV 10 2013)

Across our street a chapel with a concrete cross.
If this cross couldn't endure Yolanda …
And then, in the blink of an eye, it collapsed.
My head filled with dreadful things that might happen.

Suddenly, water from the roof deck
cascading down the stairs like a waterfalls.
We couldn't control the water coming inside.
We were left with no choice at all but to stop.
And pray.
Just pray.

Our gate pinned to the ground, none of it stood.
One of our neighbors hiding behind a post on our porch. Our porch!
We opened the doors, and what I saw …
people rushing inside, running for their lives,
faces I didn't recognize, holding hands, crying, crawling
        on the ground,
chilling, wet, soaked to the skin, hungry, bleeding, wounded.

One thing I couldn't forget—
drowning victims, kids, their lips already bluish, cold, hypothermic
I resuscitated them, tried to save them,
they were already …

They died in our basement.
It was all too late, too late.
Everything happened too fast.
We were all taken by surprise.

THE BARGE (JULITO SANCHEZ, 48, LABORER, ANIBONG, NOV 9, 2013)

The first thing I saw was the barge—

how a boat that big could get to the street

ironing down everything on its path

houses people our church

not a single post was left everything

washed away by the surge replaced

by tons and tons of debris and dead bodies

three days later the streets smelled of death

the once lush mountains clear

not a single shade of green, everything

muddy brown the leaves taken away by the winds

I've never seen mountains as pale

KINGDOM COME (DULZ CUNA, ARTIST, SAN JOSE, NOV 8 2013)

we were waiting for Kingdom Come—
               waiting for the house to shake down
my daughter looked out the window—
               she couldn't see a thing, nothing
even a tree near the house—
               when it cleared she could see water
the house at the front submerged—
               many things floating on the street

the street virtually a river—
               people on the debris, rolling, dazed
they saw me staring at them—
               some of them wounded, and
"Do you have alcohol?" Like that. —
               I threw them one half bottle.
I had another small one. —
               That's that. They were wounded.

THE CAVE (SALVADORA DAGAMI, MAT WEAVER, 72, BASEY, SAMAR, NOV 8 2013)

Inside that cave, that was where we hide.
Praying, always praying, asking for God's help.
Some were sitting, their backs on the rough sharp
edges of the cave. The wind sounded
like a siren, twirling like a *buhawi*[1].
We were soaked to the skin, our clothes dripping wet,
calling, "Lord, have mercy." I was thinking
we wouldn't survive. Morning we went back
to the barangay—the houses were gone,
fallen debris, everything destroyed, all
the rice harvested before the storm wet.
Two days passed with our stomachs empty.

---

[1] *buhawi* is the Waray-waray word for tornado.

THE PEOPLE STARTED WALKING (BEATRICE ZABALA, 16, PALO, NOV 8, 2013)

the people started walking finding their way

through the rubbles looking underneath the pile

of rubbles my uncle carried my sister

and my cousin the water was knee-level

news about an approaching tsunami

the people were panicking trying to find

a higher ground we searched for a place

which still has a second floor the wind

was still strong enough to topple us over

the people were running and we had to walk

slowly we were trudging on debris woods

with nails broken glass steel aluminum roofs

everything sharp and we were barefoot

the road covered with rubbles the only place

intact was the seminary people gathered

in that place stunned like zombies their faces

blank wet sobbing crying hungry

and unsure of the days to come

FOOD (ARNALDO PADER, 69, BARANGAY CAPTAIN, BASEY, SAMAR, NOV 12, 2013)

Days passed and nothing to eat.
On the third day we resorted to *palawan*[2],
we were left with no choice.

Anything, anything edible, we eat.
We walked from barangay to barangay,
looking for stores, for food.

We even reached Barangay Legazpi.
Good thing, my relative gave us two sacks of rice
and not long after,

my child arrived from Manila
with three and a half sacks of rice and sardines.
Our situation back then, it was really hard—

looking for food, building temporary shelters.
But help came, rice, sardines.
We survived.

---

[2]*Palawan* is a staple root crop in Eastern Samar.

LOST (DULZ CUNA, ARTIST, SAN JOSE, NOV 10, 2013)

my books, oh my god, my paintings—
                          all waterlogged, the ones here lost
but what was really lost, I was looted—
                          all my precious treasures, materials
everything was taken, even my clothes—
                          my mother's treasures, porcelain
from around the world, it was scary—
                          traumatic, my records, my music

they were watching when we went out—
                          they looted up and down, nothing
was saved, everything of the past—
                          of heritage has been looted
I know these people, they are just—
                          people from over there, but poor
they were also ravaged, but it was—
                          I was able to save my laptop

LOOTING (FATHER HECTOR, SAN JOSE, NOV 12, 2013)

I'm not going to justify the looting.
Looting in any form is a crime.
Whatever justification you make

will still be sinful in the eyes of the church.
But the looting happened. We cannot deny that.
Even some people here were doing it.

They were hungry. And the government
was slow to respond. So left on your own,
what will you do? We were on survival mode.

But the other things looted—jewelry
motorcycles appliances—that is
beyond comprehension. It happened,

it happened. Yes we are guilty of stealing!
But we cannot condemn everyone.
Those who looted for food committed

a crime, they committed a sin,
but for survival, their culpability
is lesser, that's the only thing I can say.

THE DAYS AFTER (DR ROSARIO LATORRE, TACLOBAN NOV 12 2013)

Sunday the roads were full of rubbles
and dead bodies.
It was impossible to go through.
Then came Monday—

the hospital, wounded everywhere.
No electricity, no water, no medical supplies,
no staff, and a sign at the entrance:
"NO ADMISSION. ALL SUPPLIES CONSUMED"

LOOTING II (LAURA AGOSTO, WIDOW, SAN JOSE, NOV 9— 12, 2013)

All the food that we bought got washed out by
Yolanda. My auntie's rice was mixed with
the black water from the typhoon, she just
washed it many times and then she cooked it.
And when she cooked it I was like, "Auntie,
oh my God." I swallowed the first spoon, but
I couldn't tolerate it anymore.
So we went looting, then we cooked.

For two days we looted at the BMC[3]
near Patio Victoria. Groceries,
rice, nails, hardware, napkins. Lots of things
to be looted there. I brought 30 kg
of spaghetti to the house of my auntie
and stayed there for three days. So we cooked
spaghetti noodles. Spaghetti in the
morning, noon, and macaroni at night.

We looted the BMC for sardines, corned beef,
and we cooked it without tomato sauce,
just water. The water in their tank was
preserved and cool at that moment, the flood
did not go in the tank so we could still
cook food. Even salt we didn't have -- most
of it was wet, or washed out by Yolanda.
We mixed the sardines and corned beef with soy sauce

since we looted soy sauce. My aunt cooked
rice, and we took turns in cooking other things
and then because we were only looting

---

[3]Burauen Marketing Corporation

we didn't have food to eat. What we looted
we cooked and after three days, we were looting
again. We saw rice grains that were not yet
milled stocked there in the BMC. I asked
the one who was looting the rice and rice grain,

"Can we get a sack of rice?" And he replied,
"Oh yes, just ask the owner." He pointed
to the owner, just a dead body there.
The debris and the roofs were already
going down, and underneath were candies,
biscuits, peanuts, can goods, spaghetti, so
we were selecting food which wasn't wet,
so we could put it in the plastic bag.

We reached down to the food and sometimes
I could feel a dead body and I'd run
to the other side of the warehouse where
there was cigarettes, insecticides, powder,
and napkins. We went there because we were
afraid of the dead body which looked like
it was melting so we were like "Ah!"
It was decaying. So for two days we

looted there, then after that we cleaned
the house of my auntie because there was
rain pouring down everyday, ordinary
rain. We were thinking, thank God, there was
water coming from the sky, so we could
wash everything, clean the debris, the thick
mud in the house, outside and inside the house.
We were really happy that the rain came.

IF THE DEAD WERE OURS (ARCHIE ZABALA, ARTIST, 40, PALO, NOV 9-11 2013)

Out in Real Street, I saw dead bodies.
I asked the man I met from Magallanes,
"How is it there, Mano[4], are there dead there?"

At Ceres', a dead child munched on by a dog,
and farther out there were two dead.
"Don't ask if there are dead," he replied,

"ask if there are still people alive."
There in Marasbaras, it smelled really bad.
In Pawing. Especially on the fourth day.

And at that corner was another dead
the relatives left. The dead were just placed there.
That was why when you see the dead

it already seemed normal from your viewpoint.
But they were not our dead.
Whenever we would arrive somebody would say

that we have dead. I would ask
if they drowned at sea or whatever else.
I would go and see if the dead were ours.

Someone met me telling me that our dead were many,
and only then I saw five of the dead as ours.
Nay Uday, Mariel, Odet, then Nanay[5].

---

[4]Older Brother
[5]Mother

Our dead, we would roll them in a cloth
and Nay Uday, I didn't even see her face.
When I held her foot, my hand slid so a sheet was needed.

We had to wear masks because it smelled really bad.
We wrapped her body in cloth—uncovered
it would emit a foul odor.

When we lift Nay Inday,
something comes out of her mouth, like bubbling,
a bad smell.

Odet was already dead,
her stomach bloated,
and something black on her.

Mariel was from U.P. Do you know her?
She was the one with a wound on her back
and she didn't smell that bad.

The others—Mana Inday, Uday …
Mariel was still alive after the typhoon,
what killed her was the wound on her back.

Our dead would be carried by pedicab,
tied on like wood.
I could no longer go there.

BODIES (FATHER HECTOR, SAN JOSE, NOV 10, 2013)

I saw a lot of dead people being brought to the Barangay Hall,
some still dripping with blood, fresh bodies, bloated bodies, children.
I started blessing them as I passed by.

Some people brought dead bodies to the funeral home.
And more dead bodies piled up in that triangle,
so people would see them hoping the bodies would be picked up.
They were not wrapped in body bags,
they were wrapped in blankets or covered with boxes or mats—
anything that their living relatives could find.
I remember a mother, sitting there,
never allowing herself to be separated from
        the body of her daughter.
I told her, "Go home. Somebody will take care of the body."
She said, "No. I will not go home until they pick up
        the body of my daughter."

The people were zombie-like, having blank stares.
They just walked around, not knowing what to do.
But I didn't really see a lot of 'crying'.
Probably they run out of tears?
They were just staring blankly and looking for relatives,
dead bodies of their relatives.

HOPE (SALVADORA DAGAMI, MAT WEAVER, 72, BASEY, SAMAR, NOV 8 2013)

I'm old now—gone are the days when I was
one of the fastest weavers.

When I was young, weaving was my passion.
Now my bones are weak, my sight blurry, my movements slow.

Now, after the storm hit us, we are thankful.
We were given food. We were given seedlings.

We started to plant crops and vegetables,
me and my husband. We are both weak now.

We plant, we harvest, we have food to eat.
That is our only hope.

Tim Tomlinson was born in Brooklyn, and raised on Long Island, where he was educated by jukeboxes and juvenile delinquents. He dropped out of high school on his sixteenth birthday and began a period of five years of directionless but purposeful drifting that continues to inform his fiction and poetry. He has lived in Boston, Miami, the Bahamas, New Orleans, London, Florence, Shanghai, Cha'am, and Manila. He is a graduate of Columbia University's School of General Studies (BA), and its School of the Arts (MFA). He began visiting the Philippines with his wife, Deedle Rodriguez-Tomlinson, who's from Manila, in 2003. They worked together, with the help of many others, on gathering the material for this collection. Tomlinson is a co-founder of New York Writers Workshop, and co-author of its popular text, *The Portable MFA in Creative Writing*. His full-length collection of poems, *Requiem for the Tree Fort I Set on Fire* (Winter Goose Publishing) is due in Fall 2016. His short fiction has been anthologized in *Long Island Noir* (Akashic Books), and *Fast Food Fiction Delivery* (Anvil Publishing). His stories and poems have been published in China, the Philippines, and in numerous venues in the US. Currently he resides in Brooklyn with his wife. He teaches in New York University's Global Liberal Studies program.